This Place Sucks Because of

YOU

12 Toxic Archetypes That

Make Work

Miserable

Published by SHO-TEK LLC

www.sho-tek.com

This page left intentionally blank to preserve plausible deniability.

Introduction: Well, Here We Are

Did you buy this book with someone in mind?

Did someone buy this book with *you* in mind?

I created this leadership book for the person holding it: you. I understand that when reading the title, it is natural that people *other than you* come to mind more readily. That seems normal, mostly.

Whether you bought this book, someone gave it to you, or you found it on the bus, it's now with you. And you're still reading. That means you're at least mildly curious about what's on these pages. If things are tough at work, could things be better?

Could *you* be better?

Is it bold of me to ask? Sure.

Is it a fair question? Probably.

This Place Sucks Because of YOU isn't a feel-good leadership book filled with vague affirmations and platitudes to help you be the best cheerleader for your team.

I also want to be clear that This Place Sucks Because of You is not a feel-bad leadership book, where I'm finger-wagging at the toxic archetypes as ill-intentioned, agenda-toting jerks.

The goal of This Place Sucks Because of YOU is for *you* to examine *your* behavior, which may be uncomfortable for you. Again, that's normal, mostly.

All employees participate in and contribute to the culture of an organization, with leadership modeling the idealized behaviors and values personified. The truth is, if your workplace sucks, it doesn't just *happen*.

If dysfunction is thriving, it reflects poorly on leadership.

That's you.

Disclaimer [Not Legally Binding, Sorry]

This book could offend someone.

It might be you, or someone like you.

You, or people around you, might feel called out, exposed, maybe even a little pissed off.

That's good, it means we have a starting point!

This book may seem controversial in that it aims to expose and address damaging behavior that makes a workplace more difficult than it needs to be. While there is always a cadre of people in an organization willing to participate in some self-improvement for the greater good (thank you, HR!), more likely, there are leaders in your organization who need this book to show up on their desk unannounced and with zero attribution.

This book confronts uncomfortable behaviors and situations, asking you to reflect on your role. There's no shiny cure-all, only a reality check for anyone brave enough to admit they might be part of the problem.

If you're looking for gentle guidance that respects everyone's feelings, this book may not be for you.

But if you're tired of watching dysfunction win:

Welcome. Let's get to work.

Meet the Twelve Toxic Archetypes

You and your organization are not alone. There is commonality in toxic archetypes across industries, business types, and sizes. No corporate model is immune to the forces dragging workplaces into mediocrity. These 12 toxic archetypes are the walking red flags that you've either tolerated, enabled, or *been* at some point. You'll recognize them. You may even write one of their performance reviews. One or two of them may still show up in the mirror when you're brave enough to look.

1: The Micromanaging Control Freak

"If I don't check every detail myself, it won't be right."

-You, probably.

The Story

Emma was one of your best hires. Smart, capable, a natural problem-solver. In her first six months, she redesigned a key process, improved turnaround time by 22%, and gained the trust of your most cynical stakeholder.

Now? She's quiet. Measured. Careful. She doesn't offer ideas unless prompted. And when she does, she wraps them in caveats and apology language.

Because every time she tried to take initiative, you edited it. You polished it. You just wanted to be sure. You asked for updates daily, then hourly. You wordsmithed her emails. You made her dry-run the PowerPoint slides with you before presenting them to the team, even though she had built the deck and prepared all the talking points.

Eventually, Emma stopped driving. And now you're frustrated that she no longer takes ownership of her work.

You didn't hire Emma for her potential. You hired her to become another pair of hands you could control. And the worst part? You don't even realize you're doing it.

Why It Happens

Micromanagement is usually not about standards or perfectionism, although it may appear that way from the outside. More often, it stems from fear. You might fear that if something goes wrong, it will reflect poorly on you. Delegating can feel like giving up the expertise and value that got you promoted in the first place. There's sometimes a worry about becoming unnecessary; if others can do the work, what exactly is your role?

Your way of doing things feels right to you, making it hard to trust different approaches. Past experiences can also play a role. Maybe you were burned by delegation before, or you grew up in environments where maintaining control felt like the safest approach. These patterns often develop for understandable reasons, even when they don't serve you well in leadership roles.

Companies sometimes accidentally encourage this behavior. They often promote technical experts to management positions without providing leadership training, leaving people to figure out management through trial and error. Organizations that create cultures of blame, where mistakes get punished publicly, can make delegation feel risky.

Some companies reward leaders who "know everything" about their team's work, which can encourage over-involvement. When organizations fail to define clear success metrics, managers might focus on controlling the process instead of measuring outcomes. Time pressures can also make delegation feel riskier than just doing things yourself, especially when deadlines are tight.

Notice the irony: the more you try to control everything, the less you lead. You become a bottleneck instead of a capability amplifier. When you handle too much yourself, no one else gets to develop judgment, take ownership, or build confidence.

But regardless of the reasons behind it, micromanagement creates a cascade of problems that hurt everyone.

The Real Damage

Team members may reduce their effort when they know their work won't stand on its own. Some become dependent on your approval for decisions they could handle independently. Fresh ideas get stifled when suggestions for improvement consistently get "corrected" rather than explored.

Constant oversight can make competent individuals feel less capable than they actually are. This frustration hits hardest with experienced team members who see their expertise dismissed or underutilized.

You end up working harder than everyone else, yet you receive diminishing returns. Over-involvement in tactical details prevents you from focusing on strategic opportunities. You realize you're managing tasks rather than leading people.

Reflection Questions

When's the last time you were genuinely surprised by a team member's solution to a problem?

How would team confidence change if they knew you trusted their judgment?

What could you accomplish if you weren't busy managing everyone else's tasks?

And Why Is *This* Book on *Your* Desk Again?

Did someone quietly slip this book into your office? Was it left next to your five-page comment memo on someone else's two-paragraph proposal?

Was it bookmarked at this chapter by your most capable team member, the one who's been unusually quiet in meetings lately?

If so, now you know why.

The discomfort of recognition is the first step. The more complex work comes next.

Shifting Your Mindset

The goal isn't just to stop micromanaging. It's to become the kind of leader who amplifies others' capabilities instead of constraining them.

Consider coming clean about your tendency to over-control work by actually saying the words: "I realize I've been micromanaging, and I want to change that." It's uncomfortable, but acknowledging the pattern openly creates accountability and shows that change is genuinely possible.

Once you've established that foundation, the real work begins with boundaries. You need to be specific about what truly requires your input versus what can be handled independently by the team. Resist the urge to generalize using broad categories like "important stuff" versus "routine tasks." Write down actual decisions, processes, and types of work. Then communicate these precise boundaries clearly so everyone understands the new expectations.

There will be an adjustment period, and with time, the behavior adjustment will come more naturally. That mindset change is what makes the difference between temporary behavior modification and lasting transformation.

2: The Ghost Boss

"My team knows how to find me when they need me."

– You, last week, somewhere between four back-to-back Zoom calls and an airport lounge.

The Story

Meet Aaron.

Aaron manages a critical function in your organization. Or at least, that's what his job title says. He hasn't attended a team meeting in three weeks. When he does appear, it's fifteen minutes late with an apologetic wave and some small talk before he disappears to "jump on another call."

His calendar is a wall of gray blocks marked "Executive Sync" and "Strategic Planning." His permanent chat status is "in a meeting," and his email replies often come days later, with responses like "Let's circle back on this" or "Can you handle this one?"

Meanwhile, his direct reports have questions about priorities and budget approvals. They're making educated guesses about what matters most this quarter. Two projects sat stalled waiting for his sign-off. The team submitted a process improvement proposal weeks ago, which received no acknowledgement.

Sarah, his top performer, just submitted her resignation. No exit interview planned. Aaron learned about it through a forwarded HR email and responded with: "Sorry to see her go. Can someone cover her accounts?"

The remaining team members are either working extra hours to compensate or quietly checking out because they've lost faith in getting the support they need. But Aaron's still getting praised in leadership meetings for "developing an autonomous team."

Why It Happens

Ghost Bosses often start with good intentions. Many are consciously trying to avoid micromanagement, but they sometimes swing too far in the opposite direction, failing to find the right balance. They want to trust their team and focus on strategy, believing that operational involvement might be beneath their level of responsibility.

Some individuals become preoccupied with managing upward, prioritizing visibility with senior leaders over supporting their direct reports. The busier they get with high-level meetings and initiatives, the easier it becomes to assume their team can handle things without much input. Sometimes it's simply overwhelming. When team management feels messy or time-consuming, it can be tempting to focus on work that feels more straightforward.

Organizations sometimes accidentally encourage this pattern. They reward "strategic thinking" without clearly defining what good team leadership looks like on a day-to-day basis. Many companies promote high performers without providing management training, leaving people to figure out leadership through trial and error. When performance measurements focus heavily on individual contributions rather than team development, supporting others becomes less important than achieving personal success.

Some organizations create competing priorities that constantly pull leaders away from their teams. Cultures that celebrate being "busy" can make absence feel like a sign of importance rather than a leadership gap. When companies normalize constant meetings and strategic initiatives as the primary work of leaders, direct team support can become optional.

Ghost Bosses convince themselves they're empowering people when, in reality, they might actually be leaving them without the needed guidance. They think they're avoiding micromanagement, but they could be avoiding management entirely. They believe they're trusting their team, but authentic trust in a leadership context requires engagement, not just the absence of distrust.

True empowerment needs support. Autonomy works better with appropriate guidance. Trust develops through consistent presence, not through distance.

The Real Damage

Without regular check-ins and guidance, team members become confused about priorities and make decisions in isolation. When they can't get clarity or support, some abandon initiative entirely. Others compensate by working extra hours, while some disengage.

Career development stagnates without coaching and feedback. Team members often feel disconnected from the organization's goals and are unsure whether their work aligns with expectations. Communication breakdowns create blind spots that hurt decision-making across the board.

Top talent leaves for organizations where they feel genuinely connected to leadership. Critical decisions get delayed when your input is needed but unavailable. Opportunities slip away when quick responses are required, but are too difficult to obtain.

Reflection Questions

What would your peers say about your availability?

How often do your people have to explain delays by saying they couldn't reach you?

When did you last learn something surprising about the team's actual challenges?

And Why Did This Chapter Sound Awfully Familiar?

Did this book appear after a leadership meeting where you had to ask "What's the status on..." for every project because you genuinely didn't know?

Did someone leave it in your inbox after you missed another team meeting due to "conflicting priorities"?

Did your most capable team member walk away with no explanation, leaving you wondering what you missed?

If so, your absence speaks louder than any strategy you've been working on.

The discomfort of recognition is the first step. The real work is showing up consistently.

Becoming Present

The goal isn't only to be more available. It's to become the kind of leader who amplifies and augments capabilities through engaged support rather than distant oversight.

Start by acknowledging the gap directly. Say something like: "I know I haven't been as present as you've needed me to be. I want to understand how that's affected your work." Listen to what they tell you without defending your absence or explaining all the strategic work you've been doing.

Once you've cleared the air with the team, take a good look at where you are really spending your time. Look at your calendar honestly and ask: how much of this truly requires my specific expertise, and how much could be delegated or declined?

Create space for predictable rhythms for team interaction. Block time for weekly one-on-ones with each direct report and a team meeting. Protect that time as fiercely as you would your client meetings. Make your availability predictable by establishing specific hours when people know they can reach you for non-emergency questions.

 Ultimately, when you are present and engaged with the team, you illuminate the path for the collective growth and success of your team.

3: The Credit Thief

"It was a team effort. But I led the charge."

– You, in the executive debrief,
surrounded by people who did the actual
work.

The Story

Your team narrowly pulled off a high-risk, high-visibility project. It required late nights, weekend calls, two close calls with legal review, and a last-minute pivot that only worked because someone was courageous enough to challenge your original plan.

The final presentation is today. The slide deck? Built by Maria over three sleepless nights. The data analysis? Compiled by James, who discovered the key insight everyone's talking about. The client relationship that made it all possible? Cultivated by Sam through months of careful attention.

You give the presentation. After all, you're the leader.

You thank "the team" in one breath and pivot to "what I knew we had to do" in the next. You claim you "drove alignment," "made the tough calls," and "navigated the chaos." You mention how "my experience with similar projects" informed the strategy.

You don't mention Maria by name, or the 72-hour sprint she pulled to rebuild the financial model. You don't mention James, whose competitive analysis became the foundation of your positioning strategy. You don't mention Sam, who talked the client off the ledge when your initial timeline proved impossible.

In the Q&A, when the CEO asks about the innovative approach, you say, "Well, I've been thinking about this problem differently for a while. The team did a great job executing the vision."

Later, you hear through back channels that the team feels frustrated. Some are quietly updating their resumes. You're confused because you did say it was a team effort, right?

What you missed: they needed to hear their names. Their specific contributions. Their individual value. Instead, they got absorbed in your success story.

Why It Happens

Credit theft rarely looks like declaring "I did everything myself." Usually, it's much more subtle. Sometimes it stems from insecurity about your own value, where there's a fear that sharing credit might diminish your importance to the organization. Many leaders learned this behavior by watching others who took credit for their work, creating a cycle where it feels normal.

There can be a fundamental misunderstanding about what leadership means. Some people believe their job is to be the star of every success story, rather than the person who helps others shine. There's also a natural bias that many of us have toward our own contributions. You may believe you contributed more to a project than you actually did, making it reasonable to position yourself as the primary driver.

Performance pressure can also play a role. When you feel you need to justify your position, you become compelled to connect to every success. The corporate environment often reinforces this by celebrating individual leaders rather than the teams they lead.

Organizations sometimes accidentally encourage this behavior through their systems and culture. Performance reviews that focus on individual achievement rather than team development can make personal credit seem more valuable than helping others succeed. Leadership visibility programs that consistently showcase individual executives can reinforce the idea that leaders should be the face of all wins.

When promotion criteria emphasize personal accomplishment over team growth, it sends a message about what really matters. Meeting cultures where only senior people deliver presentations, regardless of who actually did the work, can make credit absorption feel normal. Recognition systems that flow upward to leadership but rarely outward to individual contributors can make it seem like that's how organizations work.

The dangerous spiral develops gradually. When leaders consistently absorb credit, teams start holding back their most innovative ideas because sharing them feels risky. Collaboration can turn into competition for recognition rather than cooperation toward shared goals. High performers may start protecting their work instead of focusing on team outcomes, while the leader becomes dependent on others' ideas and presents them as their own insights.

The Real Damage

Motivation plummets when individuals witness others claiming their work, even if it occurs only once. Why excel if someone else gets recognition? Team members hold back creative solutions and begin doubting their own value when their specific achievements go unacknowledged.

Limited recognition hampers advancement opportunities and career development, which becomes particularly damaging for ambitious contributors who need visibility to progress in their roles.

Team members often protect their work instead of sharing it for the collective benefit, leading to competition within the team for scarce recognition. At the same time, your best contributors seek organizations that properly acknowledge their contributions.

Reflection Questions

When you tell success stories, who are the heroes? Is it usually you?

Do team members receive invitations to meetings discussing their work?

How often do senior leaders hear directly from your individual contributors?

And Why Did This Chapter Hit a Little Too Close to Home?

Did this book appear after a leadership meeting where you received praise for your team's work, and you didn't correct the record?

Was it left on your desk after your third presentation, where you failed to mention Maria's breakthrough analysis?

Did you find it bookmarked at this chapter by someone who's stopped volunteering for high-visibility projects?

If so, who might be watching to see what kind of leader you choose to be?

Sharing the Spotlight

The goal isn't just to stop taking credit. It's to become the kind of leader who actively amplifies others' contributions and helps others shine.

Start by acknowledging the pattern honestly. Start a conversation where you say something like: "I realize I haven't been good at highlighting your individual contributions when our team does well. I want to change that", which creates accountability and shows them that recognition matters to you.

In the future, restructure how you share successes. Lead with team contributions rather than your strategic overview. Use specific names and specific contributions in all communications. Instead of saying "we developed a solution," try "[Name] developed the solution that..." or "[Name]'s analysis showed that..." This shift makes individual value visible rather than absorbed.

Create opportunities for your department to present directly to senior leadership. Include attribution in all presentations showing who contributed what. When you receive credit for teamwork, immediately redirect it: "Actually, that was [Name]'s insight. You should hear more about their approach from them directly."

Build recognition into your regular processes. Require attribution in all project documentation. Create regular opportunities to spotlight individual team member innovations. Make team member recognition a standard part of your reporting.

Making significant improvements to how you recognize others will be a welcome change for those who've felt it missing. That shift from self-promotion to team development makes the difference between being a leader people work for and being a leader people want to work for.

4: The Drama Magnet

"I just want to make sure we're all aligned. But did you hear what happened in marketing?"

— You, stirring the pot with a smile.

The Story

Denise thrives on chaos. And somehow, chaos seems to follow her everywhere.

She doesn't create conflicts through confrontation. Instead, she plants seeds that grow into full-blown team wars. A casual comment to Jake about how Sarah "seemed frustrated" in yesterday's meeting. A concerned observation to Maria that "some people think the new process isn't working." A helpful heads-up to Tom that "there's been discussion about his presentation style."

None of these observations is necessarily false. But they're inflammatory interpretations of everyday workplace moments, delivered with just enough emotional weight to create anxiety and suspicion.

She feeds on the resulting drama. When Jake starts avoiding Sarah because he's worried about her "frustration," Denise is there to offer support and gather more ammunition. When Maria becomes defensive about process feedback, Denise sympathizes, but this only stirs additional doubt. When Tom gets paranoid about his communication skills, Denise provides reassuring comfort that somehow makes things worse.

You notice the increased tension but can't trace it back to any specific incident. Meetings that once ran smoothly now have underlying currents of suspicion. Team members who collaborated easily now seem to second-guess each other. Projects stall because people are walking on eggshells around perceived sensitivities.

Meanwhile, Denise positions herself as the helpful mediator, offering to "talk to people" and "smooth things over." She becomes indispensable because she's always willing to manage the conflicts she helped create. And you reward her efforts because she genuinely seems to care about team harmony.

Why It Happens

Leaders enable drama creation because they mistake emotional intensity for engagement and confuse conflict mediation for valuable contribution. When someone like Denise offers to "help with team dynamics," it feels like problem-solving rather than problem creation.

Each conflict Denise brings to your attention becomes evidence that requires active management and intervention. The emotional volatility makes quiet periods feel like you're missing something important.

Drama magnets thrive when you confound activity with productivity. They offer you "people problems" to solve, which can feel more urgent than your typical work.

Organizations accidentally encourage this behavior when they reward leaders who seem highly engaged with team dynamics, without distinguishing between healthy conflict resolution and drama amplification. Companies that avoid direct feedback about interpersonal behavior create an environment where emotional manipulation can flourish unchecked.

Some leaders grew up in chaotic environments where drama felt normal or even comforting. The artificial intensity created by drama magnets can feel familiar and engaging rather than exhausting and destructive.

The appeal becomes addictive when you start depending on the emotional stimulation and crisis management opportunities that drama magnets provide. They make your leadership feel necessary and valuable by creating problems that require your intervention.

The Real Damage

Team members become emotionally drained from navigating manufactured conflicts and artificial tensions. Normal workplace communication becomes anxious as people worry about how comments might be misinterpreted or used against them. The workplace feels unstable when perceived sensitivities may not even exist.

Authentic collaboration breaks down when words become ammunition. Team members avoid honest feedback or creative disagreement, having learned that any expressed concern might trigger an artificial crisis.

You waste time mediating problems that shouldn't exist while real issues get sidelined. Meanwhile, emotionally mature team members either protect themselves through disengagement or find healthier work environments elsewhere.

Reflection Questions

Do you find workplace conflict energizing rather than draining?

Are you solving more "people problems" than you were six months ago, and are those problems getting more complex?

Who always seems to be at the center of emotional conflicts while never being directly responsible for them?

And Why Did This Chapter Sound Awfully Familiar?

Did this book appear after your most emotionally stable team members started requesting transfers?

Did someone leave it after you spent another week mediating conflicts that seemed to evaporate the moment you got involved?

Was it bookmarked after you realized you're spending more time on "team dynamics" than actual team development?

Your drama magnet isn't helping you manage conflict. They're manufacturing it for their own benefit.

Starve the Drama Creation

Start by identifying who's always at the center of team conflicts without ever being directly responsible for them. Notice whether this person offers to mediate problems they somehow knew about before they became visible to you. Ask yourself whether team dynamics got more complicated after they became involved.

Stop providing the emotional investment that feeds drama creation. When someone brings you manufactured conflict, respond with: "It sounds like normal workplace communication. I trust the team to handle this professionally." Don't reward artificial intensity with crisis management attention.

Refuse to mediate conflicts that seem disproportionate to their apparent causes. When someone escalates minor disagreements into major interpersonal crises, step back rather than stepping in. Let typical workplace tensions resolve naturally, rather than turning them into managed conflicts.

Create calm consistency rather than reactive crisis management. Establish predictable responses to workplace friction that don't involve emergency interventions or special mediation sessions. Make it clear that normal professional disagreements don't require a crisis response.

Build team resilience by encouraging direct communication rather than triangulated emotional processing. When people come to you with interpersonal concerns, direct them back to each other: "Have you talked with them directly about this? Let's help you have that conversation rather than managing it for you."

Your drama magnet will likely escalate their efforts when you stop providing the attention and intervention that feeds their manipulation. As a leader, your emotional discipline is essential.

Instead of managing contrived conflicts or rumors, you create environments where authentic communication makes artificial drama unnecessary. Moving away from emotional reactivity to calm consistency builds genuine team health.

5: The Fearmonger

"I'm not here to be liked. I'm here to get results."

— You, after your third direct report quit this quarter.

The Story

People rehearse conversations before talking to you. That's the first thing you need to accept.

They message each other frantically before delivering updates. Some submit questions anonymously in team meetings because speaking up with their name attached feels too risky. When you walk into a room, ongoing conversations come to a pause. When your name appears in someone's inbox, they pause before opening the message.

You claim to value transparency and direct feedback, but when someone attempts to offer a different perspective, they encounter sharp questions that feel like interrogation. Sarcasm that lands like punishment for

25

speaking up. A look that clearly communicates displeasure with their input.

You tell people you want them to feel comfortable bringing you problems. But they hear something entirely different: mess this up and face the consequences.

Last week, when Jake mentioned that the timeline might be challenging, you responded with: "Challenging? Or are we just not managing our time effectively? Because I've seen this team deliver seemingly impossible things before. Maybe we need to discuss commitment levels."

Jake hasn't offered project insights since. Neither has anyone else.

Team meetings have become careful performances where people share only safe observations and positive updates. Problems often remain hidden until they escalate into something much more challenging to manage.

You've created an environment where self-protection takes precedence over performance. And you wonder why your results keep plateauing.

Why It Happens

Fearmongers often developed their approach in response to high-pressure environments where mistakes got punished publicly. Some cover insecurity about their own competence with aggressive confidence. Others learned that being "tough" was rewarded, while being "soft" was taken advantage of.

Past experiences shape this pattern. Maybe you were burned when you trusted others to handle critical work. You may have grown up in situations where maintaining control was the safest course of action. These responses made sense at the time, even when they don't serve you well in leadership roles.

Organizations often accidentally reward this behavior. Crisis cultures celebrate "tough" decision-making under pressure without examining how those decisions get made. Companies promote high performers based solely on individual results, without considering their impact on others. Some organizations tolerate aggressive behavior because the person delivers outcomes, normalizing intimidation as "high standards" or "direct communication."

The pattern becomes self-reinforcing. Fear-based leadership can produce short-term compliance that appears effective, characterized by quick decision-making due to people refraining from pushing back, suppressed conflict, and an apparent efficiency resulting from people avoiding complications.

But this creates a dangerous illusion. What appears to be strong leadership is actually a façade. People comply superficially while privately disengaging. Bad news gets buried until it escalates to a crisis. Teams become defensive instead of innovative.

The real damage compounds quickly. You stop receiving accurate information about problems and opportunities because people are afraid to share truths with you. Your best people leave for less stressful environments. People will discuss your leadership style, which can impact both recruitment and partnerships, as well as your reputation.

The Real Damage

When failure brings punishment, team members avoid proposing solutions that might not work. Learning stops because mistakes become disasters instead of opportunities for growth and development. Adaptation becomes impossible when acknowledging problems feels too dangerous.

Information flow breaks down as the team hides bad news from you. Surface compliance masks private disengagement. Blame becomes more important than solutions because avoiding your displeasure takes precedence over solving problems.

Constant stress affects confidence, health, and overall effectiveness. Capable individuals often start to doubt their abilities under persistent scrutiny. Your reputation becomes a recruitment liability while teams lose respect for leadership that operates through intimidation rather than inspiration.

Reflection Questions

What happens to your expression and tone when someone disagrees with you?

Do people seem energized or anxious after talking with you?

When did you last change your mind because a team member presented compelling evidence?

And Why Did This Chapter Hit So Hard?

Did this book appear after another anonymous survey filled with comments about "fear of retaliation" and "scared to be wrong"?

Did someone slip it into your inbox after a team meeting where your feedback sounded more like a cross-examination?

Did you find it on your desk after your most promising team member gave notice with no explanation beyond "pursuing new opportunities"?

Creating Safety

The goal isn't just to become less intimidating. It's to become the kind of leader people trust with their honest thoughts and best ideas.

Open the conversation by acknowledging your pattern of behavior. Say something direct like: "I'm concerned that I might be creating an environment where people don't feel safe being honest with me. Can you help me understand if that's happening?" Listen to their responses without defending yourself or explaining your intentions.

Start practicing vulnerability in small ways. Share a recent mistake you made and what you learned from it. Ask for feedback on decisions you're considering. Use language like: "I'm not sure I have this right. What am I missing?" Modeling honesty promotes feelings of safety.

Change how you respond to problems and mistakes. When someone brings you bad news, thank them first: "I appreciate you bringing this to me early." Ask curious questions instead of accusatory ones: "Help me understand how we got here" rather than "Why did this happen?" Focus on solutions: "What do we need to do now?" instead of blame: "Who's responsible for this?"

Publicly praise people who speak up with dissenting views. Share your own uncertainties and solicit feedback. Make it clear that thoughtful disagreement is valued rather than punished.

Model healthy conflict by responding to disagreement with genuine interest: "That's an interesting perspective. Help me understand your thinking." Change your mind publicly when someone presents compelling evidence. Thank people for pushing back on your ideas rather than making them regret it.

Letting go of your behavior and fearmongering tendencies will not happen overnight. However, by opening the door to allow people to disagree with you and with each other respectfully, you'll create an environment where more ideas come to the surface, which makes the difference between temporary compliance and sustained excellence.

6: The Overpromise-er

"Let's just tell them yes, we'll figure it out."

– You, moments before disappearing from
the group chat.

The Story

It started with a client pitch. Big visibility, significant revenue potential, and a room full of executives who need to be impressed.

You promised they'd have a full prototype in 30 days, complete deployment in 90, and seamless integration with all their legacy systems by Q2. Your presentation was confident and compelling, packed with ambitious deliverables that had the client nodding in enthusiastic agreement.

The team doing the work did not review the timeline or scope. But the team is brilliant! They'll figure it out.

They didn't because they couldn't.

By the time your team saw the signed contract, the deliverables were locked in, you published the timeline on the company roadmap, and the client had planned their entire digital transformation around your promises.

What followed was three months of 70-hour weeks, weekend war rooms, and increasingly creative explanations for why each milestone was sliding. Everyone on the team burned through their goodwill, their energy, and eventually their patience. Two people quit mid-project. Three others started interviewing elsewhere.

When the delivery date passed with a half-built product and a frustrated client, you called an all-hands meeting to discuss "execution challenges" and the need to "be more agile and responsive to changing requirements."

Everyone sat in stunned silence as you discussed learning opportunities and process improvements, never once acknowledging that the impossible timeline stemmed from promises you made without consulting the people who had to keep them.

They're not resistant to urgency. They're exhausted from trying to catch up to commitments they never made.

Why It Happens

Overpromising feels like leadership because it wins applause, secures deals, and creates excitement. Bold commitments make you look visionary and decisive. Saying "yes" when others hesitate can seem like the difference between winning and losing opportunities.

There's often genuine optimism involved. You believe people can achieve more than historical data suggests because you've seen them pull off difficult things before. Each successful delivery, no matter how chaotic, becomes evidence that your team "can handle anything."

Competitive pressure plays a role. Saying "no" or "let me check with my team" can feel like losing to more aggressive competitors. The immediate win of securing a deal or project feels more important than the long-term cost of unrealistic execution.

Sometimes there's a hero complex at work. You want to be the leader who says "yes" when others say "impossible." Being known as someone who "gets things done" becomes part of your identity, even when the getting done involves unsustainable heroics from others.

Some companies reward this behavior. Sales-driven cultures are known to celebrate significant commitments without considering the reality of delivery. Quarterly pressure prioritizes immediate wins over sustainable execution. Companies promote deal-makers without holding them accountable for what happens after the deal is signed.

Performance measurements that separate promise-making from promise-keeping create dangerous incentives. When the person who commits isn't the person who delivers, there's little natural feedback to calibrate promises against reality.

The escalation becomes self-reinforcing. Once you're known as someone who "gets things done," there's pressure to keep raising the bar. The real costs are hidden in burnout, turnover, and the gradual erosion of team capability, while the visible wins are celebrated and rewarded.

The Real Damage

When impossible deadlines become routine rather than the exception, teams operate in a state of permanent crisis mode, sacrificing personal time to meet commitments, while your work-life balance disappears. Planning becomes ineffective when scope and timelines shift unpredictably.

Everything becomes a rush job plagued by shortcuts and accumulated problems. Creative problem-solving disappears when urgency dominates. Quality suffers consistently when speed takes priority over sustainable practices.

Unmet promises damage client relationships and future opportunities. Burned-out teams can't compete against well-rested, sustainable competitors. Your best contributors leave for companies with realistic practices, while you become dependent on individual heroics rather than systematic excellence.

Reflection Questions

When did you last ask your team if a timeline was realistic before announcing it publicly?

Do your people see you as someone who builds confidence or someone who builds pressure?

Are you creating a sustainable high-performance culture, or a burnout factory?

And Why Is This Book in Your Inbox?

Did it appear after a project postmortem where no one made eye contact when you asked about "execution challenges"?

Did someone quietly forward it after you gave another "rally the troops" speech while they were still recovering from the last impossible deadline?

Did your most reliable team member mention they were "exploring opportunities with better work-life balance"?

The pattern is clear. The choice to change is yours.

Making Realistic Commitments: Rebuilding Trust

Learn to say, "Let me check with my team and get back to you." Practice this exact phrase until it becomes automatic. Stop committing in the moment to avoid disappointing people. Better to under-promise and over-deliver than to create another cycle of unrealistic expectations and chaotic execution.

Involving your team in timeline discussions before making any external commitments is essential. Ask "What would it take to deliver this well?" rather than "Can you deliver this by [date]?" Utilize their expertise to create realistic timelines that incorporate suitable buffers for unforeseen events.

When stakeholders want faster delivery, present clear options: "We can go faster if we reduce scope, add resources, or accept higher risk. Which would you prefer?" Make the cost of speed visible before committing to it. Obtain explicit agreement on prioritization in case of scope reduction due to urgency.

Create systems that include buffer time for unknowns. Establish team capacity limits that you won't exceed. Practice saying "no" to requests that would compromise existing commitments rather than saying "yes" and figuring it out later.

This adjustment will challenge your identity as someone who "makes things happen." Realistic timelines may cost you opportunities or make you seem less capable than aggressive competitors.

Focus your energy on ensuring your team has a realistic plan to deliver meaningful results. You and the team are successful when they meet or exceed expectations, and this is only possible when commitments are authentic.

7: The Untouchable Favorite

"It's complicated. There's history there."

– You, avoiding the obvious solution.

The Story

Everyone sees it. Everyone knows about it. And no one can change it.

Meet Jordan. Same mistakes every quarter. Missed deadlines that somehow become "shifting priorities." Client meetings where Jordan arrives twenty minutes late with coffee and no apology. Team projects where Jordan's contribution consistently becomes the bottleneck, yet also gets consistently excused.

When everyone else works late to meet a client deadline, Jordan logs off at 4 p.m. for a "family commitment." When the team discusses accountability for a failed initiative, Jordan "wasn't properly briefed on the requirements." When others face scrutiny for their decisions, Jordan's choices are often defended as "based on historical context."

Yet Jordan gets the best assignments. The executive coaching budget. Invitations to leadership off-sites. Access to client relationships that others built but somehow can't maintain.

Why? Because Jordan is "family", literally the VP's cousin. Or they live next door to the CEO. Or they've been here since the company had twelve employees and "built this place." Or they possess some undefined institutional knowledge that leadership can't risk losing.

Meanwhile, Maria works weekends covering Jordan's missed deadlines. Alex handles Jordan's difficult client conversations because Jordan "doesn't communicate well with that personality type." Sarah picks up Jordan's project management tasks because Jordan is "more of a big-picture person."

You've done nothing to change this dynamic. Everyone sees the truth clearly: people can work hard and play fair, yet still lose to someone who does neither.

Why It Happens

You protect underperformers because it feels easier than confronting individuals who are connected. The relationships seem too complicated to unravel. The political fallout appears too risky to navigate. So you choose the path that avoids immediate discomfort while creating long-term damage.

Sometimes there's genuine guilt involved. You feel responsible for someone's career or family situation. The history you share makes accountability feel like betrayal. The investment you've made in this person over the years creates a sunk cost mentality where letting go feels like admitting failure.

You convince yourself they possess irreplaceable knowledge or relationships, but you never actually document what they know or test whether their connections truly matter. The "institutional knowledge" becomes an excuse rather than a measurable asset.

Many workplaces enable this behavior by establishing unclear performance standards that permit subjective evaluation. Inconsistently enforced nepotism policies send mixed messages about what really matters. Political protection networks develop where favors and relationships carry more weight than results.

Fear of legal consequences around family connections or protected relationships can paralyze decision-making. Leaders often avoid difficult conversations, instead of properly documenting performance issues and following established procedures.

The rationalization becomes elaborate over time. You tell yourself the person is "going through a rough patch" that's lasted two years. You claim it would be too disruptive to make changes now while ignoring the ongoing disruption their poor performance creates. You focus on their intentions rather than their output.

Every day you maintain this protection, you lose credibility with the people who are actually performing. High performers begin to question whether merit matters in your organization. Standards become suggestions rather than requirements. Excellence becomes optional when mediocrity gets the same rewards.

The Real Damage

When mediocrity gets rewarded equally with excellence, motivation collapses entirely. The system feels rigged against actual performance, creating company-wide cynicism about fairness. Your strongest contributors waste their talents covering for protected incompetence.

Top talent exits for more mature environments, where performance actually drives advancement. Others work overtime compensating for protected underperformance, creating resentment and burnout. Standards decline to whatever the weakest protected link can achieve.

Political behavior increases as the relationship value exceeds the results. Word spreads about protection patterns, complicating recruitment efforts. Clients and partners notice when incompetence gets enabled rather than addressed.

Reflection Questions

Who in your company consistently gets away with things that would get others in trouble?

How many talented people have you lost while keeping one connected underperformer comfortable?

If every decision had to be justified based purely on performance data, what would change?

And Why Is This Chapter Dog-Eared?

Did you find this book opened to this chapter after your top performer submitted their resignation with one sentence: "I'll never get ahead here because I'm not related to anyone in the C-Suite."

Did it appear after another team meeting, where someone covered for Jordan's absence, while Jordan somehow earned credit for the project's success?

Was it left highlighted with phrases about "meritocracy" and "trust evaporates"?

The person you're protecting is dead weight, and that is a sure-fire culture killer.

Every day you delay action, your credibility slips away.

Rebuilding Merit-Based Culture

The goal isn't just to address one problematic person. It's about becoming the kind of leader who consistently applies standards, regardless of relationships or history.

Start by identifying who consistently underperforms but remains protected. List the specific behaviors or results that would get anyone else in trouble. Write down the excuses you've made for them over the past six months. This audit forces you to confront the gap between your stated values and actual decisions.

Document the reality objectively. Track contributions versus others' on recent projects. Note how often team members compensate for their work. Measure the time and energy spent managing around their limitations. Create the factual foundation for difficult conversations.

Have the accountability conversation directly with the individual. Schedule a performance discussion with specific examples and clear expectations: "I need to see improvement in these areas by this date. Here's what success looks like." Establish consequences: "If these changes don't happen, we'll need to make different decisions about your role."

Apply the same standards to everyone, regardless of relationships or tenure. Give high performers the same access and opportunities currently reserved for favorites. Make it clear that contribution, not connection, drives essential decisions.

Address the broader team impact by acknowledging that, from now on, consistent application of standards is the norm. Stop asking strong performers to compensate for the weaknesses of others. Create transparent processes for advancement and opportunity allocation based on measurable criteria.

The protected person may push back harder than others when finally held accountable. Other stakeholders may pressure you to maintain the status quo. The change in how you handle performance will test your commitment to fairness.

By establishing that merit matters more than relationships, you begin to lead a meritocracy. That shift from selective standards to consistent accountability makes the difference between a workplace people tolerate and one they're proud to be part of.

8: The Culture Mascot

"We're a family here. A high-performing, values-driven family."

– You, moments before voting your auntie off the island.

The Story

Your town halls are legendary. People share the recordings. They clap at your references to "collaborative excellence" and "radical candor." You've mastered the art of the inspirational quarterly kickoff, complete with personal stories about your first job and what it taught you about treating people right.

The company hoodie suits you well. Your LinkedIn posts about "putting people first" get hundreds of likes. The values deck might as well have your name on it, given how fluently you can deliver phrases about "psychological safety" and "inclusive leadership."

Then, on Monday morning, the real decisions begin.

The inspiring speech about transparency on Tuesday precedes a closed-door leadership meeting on

Wednesday to plan layoffs that will take place this Friday. Your morning email about "work-life balance" gets followed by an evening message questioning people's "dedication" because project timelines are slipping.

You roll out unconscious bias training with great fanfare, then promote your golf buddy over three more qualified candidates who happened to be women. You tell everyone "we're all in this together" during the Q3 meeting, right before approving executive bonuses while freezing merit increases for everyone else.

The team learned to decode the gap between your presentations and your decisions. Some have started calling your motivational emails "corporate poetry", beautiful language signifying nothing. They exchange knowing glances during your values presentations.

You believe you're building culture. What you're actually doing is performing it while undermining it with every contradictory choice.

Why It Happens

Culture performance feels authentic when you genuinely believe in the vision you're communicating. You truly want to create a positive culture, but you lack the skills or courage to implement it when implementation conflicts with other priorities. The inspirational messaging feels easier and more comfortable than making hard decisions that actually align with stated principles.

Image management often drives this behavior. You confuse building your reputation as a values-driven leader with actually being one. The applause and positive feedback from inspirational communications can become addictive, especially when the alternative is making difficult choices that might be unpopular.

Some leaders learned this approach by watching others who spoke brilliantly about values but acted differently in practice. It can seem like normal corporate behavior; everyone gives inspiring speeches while making expedient decisions behind closed doors.

Conflict avoidance plays a significant role. Values language feels safer than making decisions that will upset stakeholders or require difficult conversations. It's easier to talk about "putting people first" than to choose people over profits when the two conflict.

There's often pressure to inspire without corresponding pressure to implement. Some companies measure leaders on how they make people feel, rather than what they make possible, or even what they accomplish. Companies separate culture from operations, treating values as HR initiatives rather than business imperatives that should guide every significant decision.

Promotion criteria typically emphasize communication skills and strategic vision over consistency in value. Meeting cultures reward those who deliver compelling presentations, regardless of whether their actions align with their words. Recognition systems prioritize messaging ability over behavioral alignment.

The performance becomes self-reinforcing when it generates positive responses. People respond well to inspirational content, at least initially. The disconnect between words and action may not be immediately apparent, especially to stakeholders who are not directly involved in daily operational decisions.

The Real Damage

Team members become immune to inspirational messaging when leadership actions consistently contradict stated values. Positive communication gets interpreted as manipulation designed to soften unpopular decisions. Employees abandon stated values when they see leadership do the same.

Decision-making becomes confusing when teams struggle to determine which principles truly matter under pressure. Initiative and innovation decline when stated values prove to be just performance art rather than operational guidance.

Internal contradictions become external reputation problems. Word spreads about gaps between marketing and reality, making both recruitment and client relationships more difficult. Authentic competitors attract talent and customers who can distinguish between genuine values and corporate theater.

Reflection Questions

When did you last say, "this doesn't align with our values," and actually do something about it?

If someone observed only your decisions for six months, what would they conclude your actual values are?

And Why Was This Book on Your Chair?

Did it arrive after your fifth "transparency update" that revealed absolutely nothing worthwhile to anyone?

Did someone leave it near your office after another inspiring all-hands meeting where you discussed "feeling secure in your job" while everyone stayed quiet about the layoffs they knew were coming?

Your performance isn't fooling anyone anymore. The gap between inspiration and action is a chasm.

Time to choose which side you want to stand on.

Authentic Culture Building

Review the last month and identify where your actions contradicted your messages. Ask yourself honestly: where did expediency win over principles, and what message did that send?

Stop using inspirational language to soften difficult decisions. When you need to make an unpopular choice, lead with transparency about why it's necessary rather than wrapping it in motivational messaging. Let your choices stand on their own merit, rather than on your ability to package them attractively.

Choose one core value and commit to living it consistently, even when it's costly or inconvenient. Make decisions based on stated principles rather than political convenience. Test every choice against this question: "If my team could see all my reasoning, would they believe I practice what I preach?"

Create genuine transparency by sharing the reasoning behind difficult decisions, rather than just announcing the results. When expediency wins over values, acknowledge it directly: "I made this choice for business reasons, and I know it doesn't align with our commitment to X." Ask for feedback: "Where do you see gaps between what we say we value and what we actually do?"

Build accountability by asking people to point out contradictions when they see them. When you act against stated values, acknowledge it openly rather than defending or rationalizing your actions. Make values-based decision-making visible by showing when it costs you something, but you choose it anyway.

The adjustment requires confronting the difference between wanting to be seen as values-driven and actually being values-driven. Your team may initially be skeptical of changes, having learned that your words do not always predict your actions. Some stakeholders may push back when you start making expensive principle-based decisions.

Matching words and actions is a simple yet powerful concept. You're transitioning from a culture performer to a culture creator. This shift makes the difference between temporary motivation and lasting culture change.

9: The Gossip Broker (a.k.a. Poison Pill)

"People are saying..."

– You, quoting the most toxic person on your team.

The Story

You think it's just feedback. Candid. Honest. From someone who's "in the know."

They slide into your office with perfectly curated intelligence. Never dramatic. Never emotional. Just concerned, professional observations delivered with the right mix of loyalty and reluctance.

"I probably shouldn't mention this, but there's been some discussion about the new hiring strategy. Not criticism, just questions about the rationale."

"I don't want to speak out of turn, but I'm hearing the team isn't entirely confident in the Q4 projections. Maybe worth a conversation?"

"This stays between us, but there's been some concern about Sarah's client management approach. Nothing specific, just a pattern people have noticed."

It's never gossip. It's *insight*. Strategic intelligence about team dynamics, morale issues, and potential problems you need to know about. They position themselves as your cultural informant, the person who keeps you connected to the ground truth.

And you listen, because they seem uniquely plugged into information you can't access directly. They speak with authority about team sentiment, individual performance, and organizational dynamics. Their updates feel valuable and timely.

Here's what you don't notice: every piece of "intelligence" serves its agenda. Sarah, who they mention? She's up for the same promotion they want. The team's "concerns" about Q4 projections? Those doubts started after they were uninvited from the planning process. The "discussion" about hiring strategy? It began when the hiring manager didn't select their preferred candidate.

They don't create drama; they're far more devious than that. They collect, curate, and strategically deploy information to shape your understanding of reality. And you're helping them succeed by treating their manipulated intelligence as ground truth.

Why It Happens

The Gossip Broker thrives in environments where you have limited direct access to team dynamics and rely on intermediaries for organizational intelligence. They fill information gaps you should be filling yourself through direct engagement.

You get drawn into this dynamic because the information feels valuable and exclusive. When someone offers insider knowledge about team morale, individual performance, or organizational politics, it appears to be responsible leadership intelligence rather than manipulation. The intelligence is delivered professionally, with apparent concern for organizational success.

Gossip Brokers position themselves as loyal allies who help you stay informed. They wrap strategic manipulation in the language of organizational development and team support. Unlike drama magnets who create emotional chaos, they appear calm and analytical, more like internal consultants than troublemakers.

You become dependent on their intelligence because it makes you feel informed about dynamics you can't see directly. The information appears more comprehensive and nuanced than the surface-level updates typically provided in formal meetings. They provide context and interpretation that help you understand team behavior.

Organizations accidentally enable this behavior when they create information silos that make secondhand reports valuable. Poor communication systems create information gaps that gossip networks rush to fill. When you're isolated from day-to-day team interactions, you become vulnerable to anyone offering to bridge that gap.

Companies sometimes reward people who position themselves as culturally aware without distinguishing between genuine insight and manipulated intelligence. When organizations avoid addressing individual performance directly, it creates space for triangulated reporting to flourish.

The danger compounds when you start depending on their filter. The gossip broker gradually becomes your primary lens for understanding team dynamics. They don't just report on problems; they curate your entire understanding of what's happening, shaping your decisions based on their version of reality.

The Real Damage

Decision-making becomes based on filtered, biased information rather than direct observation. Personnel decisions, resource allocations, and strategic choices get made based on one person's agenda rather than objective reality.

Team members become guarded about expressing concerns, creative disagreements, or honest feedback when they realize that casual comments might be used as a means to gather intelligence. Targeted individuals suffer professional damage without understanding why their work gets scrutinized more heavily and advancement opportunities diminish.

You lose credibility when you can't distinguish between truth and manipulation. Your strongest contributors seek organizations where gossip brokers won't twist their words or manipulate their relationships. Meanwhile, the broker gains disproportionate influence while authentic contributors lose their voice.

Reflection Questions

Who brings you the most "concerns" about other people, and what do you actually know about their motivations?

How often do you verify intelligence with multiple sources before taking action?

Are people becoming more guarded around you rather than more open?

Do you feel more informed about team dynamics, or more suspicious of them?

And Why Is This Chapter Highlighted in Three Colors?

Was this book delivered anonymously, with this chapter dog-eared and a sticky note that says, "Ask around"?

Was it left on your desk after a well-liked team member resigned without warning and with no explanation beyond, "I can't anymore"?

Did you find it after realizing your most "informed" source somehow predicted every team problem while never being responsible for solving any of them?

Then here's your moment: That voice you rely on for organizational intelligence? They might be the reason you don't hear the authentic truth from anyone else.

Leadership means making decisions based on reality, not curated fiction.

Starve the Information Manipulation

The next time someone brings you secondhand "concerns," respond with: "That's worth exploring. Let's bring [person] into this conversation so I can hear their perspective directly." Don't provide the exclusive audience that feeds manipulation.

Demand specifics and accountability. When someone reports team "concerns" or individual "issues," ask for concrete examples, timelines, and measurable impacts. If they can't provide specifics, they're trafficking in manipulation, not intelligence.

Create direct access to ground truth. Establish regular communication channels with individual contributors, enabling them to share challenges without fear of retribution or triangulation. Make it clear that you prefer to hear about difficulties directly from the people experiencing them.

Build transparency around decision-making. When you receive reports about performance or team dynamics, document the source and verify the information with multiple perspectives before taking action. Make your decision-making process transparent so that people understand how you use information.

Notice patterns in *who* is targeted by the Gossip Broker's "concerns" and whether those patterns align with the Gossip Broker's interests.

The adjustment will challenge your comfort with feeling "informed." You may discover that much of your organizational intelligence was someone's self-serving and devious plotting. This uncertainty is healthier than false confidence based on strategic manipulation.

10: The Exhausted Martyr

"I haven't taken a real vacation in three years. Just doing what needs to get done."

– You, half-joking. But also fully expecting applause.

The Story

You arrive at 6 a.m. because "there's so much to get done." You eat lunch at your desk while reviewing reports. You answer emails during your commute, take calls during your kid's soccer game, and respond to messages at 11 p.m. because "the team depends on me."

You haven't used your vacation days in two years. When you got food poisoning last month, you still joined the client call from your bathroom floor because "no one else understands this account like I do."

Your calendar is a wall of back-to-back meetings with no buffer time. You regularly work through weekends, skip family dinners for "urgent" projects, and pride yourself on being the first one in the office and the last one to leave.

When Sarah leaves at 5:30 p.m. for her daughter's recital, you make a pointed comment about "dedication during busy periods." When Jake declines a weekend meeting, citing family plans, you respond with a heavy sigh and "I guess I'll handle it myself."

People stop taking lunch breaks. They apologize for being "unavailable" during evenings and weekends. They compete to see who can look most exhausted in Monday morning meetings, wearing their burnout like a badge of honor.

Maria just submitted a resignation letter citing "unsustainable work-life balance expectations." Two other team members have started showing signs of chronic stress. Productivity is actually declining despite the increased hours, but you interpret this as evidence that everyone needs to work even harder.

You think you're modeling commitment and work ethic. What you're actually modeling is dysfunction disguised as dedication.

Why It Happens

Martyr leaders often developed their approach in environments where overwork was the only path to recognition or job security. You might have learned early that being indispensable meant being valuable, and that taking breaks was a sign of weakness or lack of commitment.

Some leaders use exhaustion as a means to prove their importance. If you're constantly overwhelmed, it must mean you're essential to organizational success. The busier you appear, the more valuable you feel, creating an addictive cycle where rest feels like irrelevance.

Past experiences can shape this pattern. Maybe you survived layoffs because you were the person who never said no to additional work. You may have received praise for heroic efforts during crises, making crisis-level intensity feel normal and necessary.

There's often genuine anxiety about delegation or team development. If others can handle the work effectively, what happens to your role and value? Maintaining control over everything provides certainty, even when it's unsustainable.

Organizations frequently reward this behavior without recognizing its costs. Companies celebrate leaders who are "always available" and "never miss a deadline." They promote people who sacrifice personal time for organizational goals without measuring the long-term impact on team health or sustainable performance.

Performance cultures that equate hours with dedication create environments where visible exhaustion becomes a competitive advantage. When organizations lack clear productivity metrics, time invested can become a proxy for value delivered.

The pattern becomes self-reinforcing when your identity becomes tied to being the person who sacrifices the most. Your worth gets measured by your willingness to give up personal time and boundaries. Rest starts feeling selfish, and sustainable practices seem like a sign of laziness.

The dangerous escalation happens when your team begins mirroring your behavior to avoid seeming uncommitted. What started as your personal work style becomes the cultural standard for everyone.

The Real Damage

Teams operate under constant stress, always ensuring they appear busy and committed enough. Necessary breaks, vacation time, and recovery periods often get put on the back burner because they seem less important than what leadership feels is necessary.

Performance decreases when exhaustion becomes chronic. Tired individuals make more mistakes, solve problems more slowly, and struggle with creative thinking. Work quality suffers even as hours increase.

Your best contributors seek organizations with sustainable practices. Family relationships, health, and personal well-being deteriorate not just for you, but for everyone pressured to keep up with your unsustainable pace. The organization develops a reputation for burnout, which limits its ability to attract quality talent.

Reflection Questions

What are you modeling: sustainable high performance or unsustainable martyrdom?

Do you respond respectfully or resentfully when someone enforces boundaries?

Are you creating a culture where people feel guilty for taking care of themselves?

What could your team accomplish if they didn't overwork?

And Why Did This Chapter Arrive With a PTO Request Form?

Was this book left on your desk right after a team member took their first vacation in two years and returned to find twice the workload waiting?

Did it appear after your fourth "just one quick thing before you log off" email this week?

Did you find it after realizing your team's sick days have tripled and their engagement scores have plummeted?

If so, your approach to work isn't inspiring dedication; it's creating damage.

Building Sustainable Excellence

The goal isn't just to work fewer hours. It's to become the kind of leader who demonstrates that high performance and healthy boundaries can coexist.

Start by acknowledging the pattern. Say something direct like: "I realize I've been modeling unsustainable work habits, and I'm concerned about the pressure I've created for all of you. I want to change that." Listen to what they tell you about the real impact of your approach.

Take visible time off and communicate the boundaries clearly. Use your vacation days, disconnect completely during off-hours, and stop responding to non-urgent communications outside of business hours. Make these changes visible so people understand they have permission to do the same.

Redefine dedication from hours worked to outcomes achieved. Start measuring and celebrating results rather than hours spent. Recognize people for efficient problem-solving, not for staying late. Make it clear that working smarter is more valuable than working longer.

Build systems that don't depend on your constant availability. Document processes, cross-train team members, and establish clear decision-making authority so work can progress even when you're not present. Institute redundancy that makes the organization more resilient and less dependent on individual heroics.

Set explicit expectations about work-life boundaries. Inform the team that you expect them to utilize their vacation time, respect their own personal time off, and prioritize sustainable practices. Make boundary-setting a performance expectation, not just a nice-to-have benefit.

The adjustment will challenge your identity and your assumptions about what makes you valuable. You may worry that working sustainable hours will make you seem less committed or essential. People may initially test the new boundaries, uncertain whether the changes are genuine or temporary.

By changing how you model work practices, you're shifting from crisis-driven leadership to sustainable high performance. Instead of measuring success by sacrifice, you start measuring it by consistency. That shift from martyrdom to sustainability makes the difference between short-term heroics and long-term organizational health.

11: The Conflict Avoider

"I don't like to micromanage. I trust people to work things out on their own."

– You, moments before pretending not to hear someone cry in a meeting.

The Story

You noticed it happening gradually, and you hoped it would resolve itself.

Sarah had always been direct, but lately her feedback was becoming sharp and dismissive. When Jake tried to explain project delays, she'd cut him off with "That sounds like excuses" or "We need solutions, not problems." When Maria suggested alternative approaches, Sarah would respond with visible eye rolls and comments like "I guess we can try that if you think it'll work."

The team dynamic began shifting. People became quieter when Sarah spoke. Jake started sending you private messages instead of bringing up concerns in meetings. Maria requested to work from home more frequently, citing better focus. Other team members began arriving late to meetings where they knew Sarah would be present.

You could see the tension building in awkward pauses and careful language, but you told yourself it was temporary. Sarah was a strong performer who delivered results and maintained good client relationships. The situation felt complicated, and you didn't want to make things worse by stepping in inappropriately.

You hoped the team would work things out naturally. After all, these were smart, professional people who should be able to navigate interpersonal challenges without management intervention.

However, Jake then submitted his resignation with little explanation beyond "personal reasons." Maria requested a transfer to another team. Two other team members began showing signs of disengagement, completing only the minimum required work, and avoiding collaboration.

When you finally conducted exit interviews, the feedback was clear: "I couldn't work in that environment anymore, and it was obvious that management wasn't going to address it."

The issues hadn't resolved on their own. Your avoidance had allowed a toxic dynamic to spread, ultimately costing you good people and damaging team performance.

Why It Happens

Conflict Avoiders often developed their approach in chaotic environments where stepping into conflict made situations worse. If you grew up in volatile households or workplaces, you learned that keeping quiet was safer than risking escalation. These survival instincts, once protective, can become liabilities in leadership.

Many conflict avoiders genuinely care about relationships and worry that addressing problems directly might damage connections or hurt people's feelings. You might prefer harmony over confrontation, not realizing that avoiding necessary conflicts actually creates more harm than addressing them directly.

Sometimes the avoidance stems from uncertainty about conflict resolution skills. You'd rather not engage than risk making a situation worse, which feels responsible but often enables problems to grow. The fear of saying the wrong thing can paralyze you into saying nothing at all.

Some companies reward this approach by promoting "collaborative" leaders who appear to have no visible team problems. Companies may not realize that the absence of surface conflict indicates that issues are being pushed underground rather than resolved.

Many companies fail to provide training in "difficult conversation" skills, then wonder why their managers struggle with them. When leaders who do address conflicts get questioned or criticized rather than supported, it creates an environment where avoidance feels safer than engagement.

You convince yourself that you're enabling independent problem solving, when actually you're creating a situation where people are without the support they need. You mistake non-interference for trust, when genuine trust requires engagement and accountability.

What feels like diplomatic leadership can enable problems to metastasize. When toxic behavior goes unaddressed, it doesn't disappear. It spreads and becomes normalized, especially when you remain silent.

The Real Damage

When toxic behavior faces no consequences, team members lose faith in the leadership's ability to uphold standards and provide a safe work environment. Your top performers won't fight battles they believe you should be handling, and they'll seek out other workplaces with more effective leadership.

Communication becomes increasingly indirect as individuals work around problems instead of through them. Team members protect themselves through avoidance and disengagement rather than addressing issues directly. Your understanding of team dynamics becomes distorted because problems fail to reach you.

Turnover increases, particularly among your best contributors who have options elsewhere. New team members encounter the same unaddressed issues and either adapt to the dysfunction or leave quickly. The culture stagnates because change requires addressing conflicts you've established a pattern of avoiding.

Reflection Questions

What toxic behavior do you tolerate because confrontation makes you uncomfortable?

Who benefits from your silence, and who suffers because of it?

When people bring you problems, do they leave feeling heard or dismissed?

How many good people have you lost because you wouldn't address one problematic person?

And Why Did This Chapter Quietly Show Up in Your Bookmarked Pages?

Did someone slip you this book after you sent another vague email, hoping a "team discussion" would resolve obvious problems?

Was it left on your desk by a manager who's tired of escalating issues that disappear into your leadership black hole?

Did you find it after your most patient team member finally walked away, leaving you wondering why they never came to you directly?

If so, your avoidance isn't preserving harmony, it's enabling harm.

The problems you're not addressing are still there, getting worse every day you delay.

Leading Through Difficult Conversations

The goal isn't to become confrontational or aggressive. It's to become the kind of leader who addresses problems directly and constructively before they damage teams and drive away good people.

Start by identifying the conversations you've been avoiding. Write down the specific behaviors, situations, or conflicts that you know need attention but haven't addressed. This audit forces you to confront the gap between what you know needs to happen and what you've done.

Schedule the difficult conversation immediately. The longer you wait, the harder it is and the more damage accumulates. Prepare by focusing on specific behaviors and their impact rather than personality judgments or character assessments.

Use direct, clear language. Instead of saying "there have been some concerns about communication style," say "when you interrupt team members and dismiss their ideas, it's affecting collaboration and morale." Be specific about what needs to change and what success looks like.

Set clear expectations and consequences. Make it clear that behavioral changes are not optional. Establish timelines for improvement and follow-up meetings to assess progress. Document the conversation and the agreed-upon expectations.

Follow through consistently. If behavior doesn't improve within the agreed timeframe, take the next step rather than hoping for additional time to solve the problem. Your credibility depends on matching your actions to your stated expectations.

Support individuals affected by problematic behavior. Let them know you're aware of the situation and taking action. Rebuild trust by demonstrating that leadership will protect team standards and individual contributors.

The adjustment period will test your comfort with conflict and your resolve to maintain standards. The problematic person may push back or escalate their behavior when finally held accountable. Other team members may initially be skeptical that real change is possible.

By engaging in necessary conflicts, you're transforming from a manager who hopes problems will disappear to a leader who actively maintains team health. Instead of measuring success by the absence of visible conflict, you start measuring it by how quickly problems get addressed and resolved. That shift from avoidance to engagement makes the difference between a team that tolerates dysfunction and one that demands excellence.

12: The Proximity Politician

"I just want to stay aligned with leadership."

– You, while quietly positioning everyone else as expendable.

The Story

Meet Alex.

Alex has been with the company for eleven years, but if you ask anyone what Alex actually does, you'll get vague answers. "Strategic initiatives." "Cross-functional collaboration." "Leadership support." "Business development."

What Alex excels at is being present. Every leadership meeting? Alex is there, nodding thoughtfully and taking strategic notes. Every executive presentation? Alex contributed "key insights" to the deck, usually by wordsmithing someone else's analysis into more palatable language. Every high-visibility project? Alex is somehow credited as a "co-lead" despite doing none of the technical work.

Alex speaks fluently in executive language frameworks and strategic imperatives. They position themselves as the bridge between leadership vision and team execution, the person who "translates strategy into actionable insights."

Meanwhile, Elena has been revolutionizing your customer onboarding process. She reduced time-to-value by 40%, improved retention metrics, and built training programs that other departments want to replicate. But Elena doesn't have time for coffee chats with the C-suite or strategic off-sites. She's too busy actually solving problems and delivering results.

Guess who got promoted last quarter?

Alex now manages Elena. And three other people who do the work Alex has been taking credit for.

In your leadership team meeting, Alex presents Elena's customer success metrics as "our strategic wins in the onboarding transformation initiative." Elena's name appears once, buried in the acknowledgments slide, grouped with four other people under "thanks to the amazing execution team."

Elena submitted her resignation yesterday. Her exit interview cited "lack of recognition for contributions" and "feeling like others were appropriating my work." You're confused, after all, Alex always spoke highly of Elena and even recommended her for a performance bonus.

You missed the part where Alex systematically repositioned themselves as the strategic architect of Elena's operational success, and you, as the executive, believed it.

Why It Happens

Proximity Politicians aren't usually outright frauds. They're strategic opportunists who've learned that in many organizations, perception can matter as much as performance. They become skilled at a particular game because they've discovered that game pays off.

These patterns often develop from specific backgrounds and experiences. Some are corporate climbers who discovered early that visibility advances careers faster than productivity alone. Others might be former consultants who brought client management and presentation skills into internal roles, or people who struggled with technical execution but found they excel at narrative management.

These individuals become fluent in executive language and skilled at information arbitrage, collecting insights from those doing the work and repackaging them for leadership consumption. They learn to make their wins sound like the result of their strategic thinking and invest heavily in managing up, often more so than managing down.

Organizations sometimes accidentally reward this approach. When promotions are based primarily on leadership perception rather than measurable team impact, it favors those who excel at managing perceptions. Many companies lack clear systems for tracking individual contributions to collaborative work.

When presentation skills get valued more highly than execution excellence, it creates opportunities for those who are better presenters than producers. Performance evaluations that confuse networking ability with leadership capability contribute to this dynamic, as do information asymmetries, where leaders often rely on intermediaries to understand the realities at the ground level.

The danger escalates when proximity politicians become your primary filter for understanding organizational dynamics. They don't just redirect credit; they begin to shape your entire understanding of team performance, individual capabilities, and strategic priorities.

You start seeing the organization through their lens, making decisions based on their interpretation of events rather than direct observation or multiple perspectives.

The Real Damage

When proximity appears more valuable than performance, talented individuals question why they should strive for excellence when political positioning seems more rewarding.

Many capable team members quietly seek opportunities elsewhere, looking for organizations where actual value gets recognized and rewarded. Some stop innovating entirely, having learned that breakthrough ideas will likely get claimed by someone else.

Trust erodes when team members prioritize protecting their ideas over sharing them openly. Collaboration breaks down when working with known credit redirectors becomes risky rather than rewarding. The culture becomes more political than performance-focused, while teams lose respect for leadership that can't distinguish between substance and presentation skills.

Reflection Questions

Who gets promoted faster in your organization, your performers, or your political operators?

Are you hearing from people who are doing the work, or just from those who attend meetings about the work?

Who's shaping your understanding of what's happening on the ground, and what might their motivations be?

When you praise someone's strategic thinking, do you actually know where those ideas originated?

And Why Did This Chapter Appear After Your Last "Skip Level" Meeting?

Was this book quietly left on your desk after you praised someone whose own team privately calls them a "slide deck parasite"?

Was it bookmarked by your EA, who's watched this person forward other people's emails and repackage their insights for months?

Did you find it after realizing your most "strategically minded" leader can't answer basic questions about implementation without deflecting "execution details"?

The proximity politician isn't building organizational capability. They're building a moat around themselves while taking credit for others' work.

Creating Merit-Based Recognition

The goal isn't just to stop rewarding political behavior; it's also to prevent it. It's to become the kind of leader who recognizes actual contribution and builds systems that reward substance over presentation.

Start by auditing your information sources. Track who brings you insights into team performance, project outcomes, and strategic opportunities. Notice whether their reports consistently position themselves favorably, while others appear as "execution resources" rather than strategic contributors.

Create direct access to ground truth by establishing regular communication with individual contributors. Skip-level meetings, project retrospectives, and informal check-ins help you understand who's actually doing the innovative work versus who's repackaging it for leadership consumption.

Demand specificity in strategic discussions. When someone presents insights or recommendations, ask about the research, analysis, or creative process that led to those conclusions. Track whether they can provide details or deflect to generalities.

Build attribution into your recognition systems. Require project documentation that identifies specific contributions. Create opportunities for individual contributors to present their own work directly to leadership. When you receive strategic recommendations, insist on meeting the people who developed the underlying analysis.

Restructure meetings to include the individuals who are actually doing the work, not just those managing or presenting it, providing you with direct access to both strategic thinking and implementation reality, making political intermediaries less necessary and less valuable.

Establish advancement criteria that emphasize measurable team development and individual contributor growth rather than just strategic positioning or executive presence. Make it clear that leadership means building others' capabilities, not appropriating their contributions.

The adjustment period will reveal how much of your "strategic intelligence" was actually a result of political manipulation. Some information sources may resist when you start seeking multiple perspectives and direct access to contributors. Your most political operators may become defensive when attribution becomes more transparent.

By changing how you source information and recognize contribution, you're shifting from perception-based to reality-based leadership. Instead of rewarding those who present well, you start identifying those who actually produce results and develop the capabilities of others. That shift from political reward systems to merit-based recognition makes the difference between leading a performance theater and leading a high-performing organization.

Conclusion: You're Still Here

You made it to the end.

That means one of three things happened: you recognized yourself in these pages and kept reading anyway, someone you care about recognized you in these pages and you're trying to figure out what they saw, or you're genuinely curious about becoming a better leader.

Any of those reasons is fine by me.

If you saw yourself in these chapters and were honest during the reading, you probably did; the question isn't whether you've been one of these toxic archetypes. The question is: what are you going to do about it?

Change is hard, especially when it means admitting that your leadership style has been hurting the people you're supposed to be helping, especially when it means confronting behaviors that felt normal or even necessary in your work environment.

But here's what I know after years of watching leaders either transform or stay stuck: the ones who change are the ones who get tired of their own excuses.

They get tired of explaining why good people keep leaving.

They get tired of being the bottleneck in every decision.

They become tired of wondering why their team no longer brings them great ideas.

They get tired of working harder than everyone else while getting worse results.

They get tired of the gap between who they think they are as a leader and what their behavior demonstrates.

The Real Work Starts Now

Reading this book was the easy part. The hard part is looking in the mirror tomorrow morning and asking yourself: "What kind of leader do I actually want to be?"

And I don't mean your fancy LinkedIn profile self, I mean the leader you're going to choose to be when you're stressed, when you're behind on deadlines, when someone challenges your idea in a meeting, when you must face any uncomfortable workplace reality.

Because that's when your real leadership shows up.

A Few Things to Remember

Your team notices when your actions don't match your words. They notice when you say you value transparency but make decisions behind closed doors. They notice when you ask for feedback, but they become defensive when you receive it.

They also notice when you start doing things differently.

You don't have to be perfect. Be honest about your imperfections and committed to getting better. Your team will respect authentic effort to improve more than they'll respect polished performances of leadership.

The culture you create starts with the culture you embody. If you want psychological safety, demonstrate it. If you want innovation, reward people for taking creative risks, even when they don't yield the expected results. If you want accountability, hold yourself accountable first.

What Success Actually Looks Like

You'll know you're making progress when people start bringing you problems instead of hiding them from you.

When team meetings become places where people disagree with you, do so respectfully and directly.

When your best people stop looking for other jobs because they're excited about what they're building with you.

When you realize you're spending more time developing others than managing their every move.

When someone gives you feedback, and your first instinct is curiosity instead of defensiveness.

When you make a mistake, your first move should be to acknowledge it, rather than trying to explain it away.

The Choice Is Yours

The workplace that sucks? It doesn't have to.

However, it won't change simply because you read this book or any other book.

It will change because you decided to stop being one of them.

So, close the book.

And ask yourself: What am I going to do differently tomorrow?

The answer to that question is the difference between reading about leadership and actually leading.

Your team is waiting to see what you choose.

www.ingramcontent.com/pod-product-compliance
Lightning Source LLC
Chambersburg PA
CBHW070816280326
41934CB00012B/3195